QUICK COMFORTS

How about redecorating your bedroom this weekend? Or maybe you'd like to add a fresh splash of color to your living room in just one evening? You'll be amazed at how quickly you can crochet these fast-to-finish pillows and afghans. That's because super-bulky weight yarn and a large crochet hook make fast work of each design. The pillows can be completed in approximately three to nine hours, while the lap-size afghans are ready to use in about nine to fourteen hours! Each big, beautiful home accent will warm and refresh your haven in a hurry, leaving you with plenty of time to enjoy your new décor.

LEISURE ARTS, INC.
Maumelle, Arkansas

WINDOWPANE PILLOW

Stitched with super-bulky weight yarn for a fast-to-finish design, this pillow will be ready to enhance your home in no time. Using long double crochet stitches to create a windowpane effect, this stylish accent will make a terrific textural addition to your decor—especially when combined with its companion afghan (Shown on page 16)!

EASY +

Finished Size: 14" (35.5 cm) square

MATERIALS

SUPER BULKY 6

Super Bulky Weight Yarn
[6 ounces, 106 yards
(170 grams, 97 meters) per skein]:
- Blue - 2 skeins
- Brown - 2 skeins

Crochet hook, size N (9 mm) **or** size needed for gauge
14" (35.5 cm) Pillow form
Yarn needle

GAUGE: In pattern, 11 sts = $5\frac{1}{2}$" (14 cm);
9 rows = $4\frac{3}{4}$" (12 cm)

Gauge Swatch: $5\frac{1}{2}$"w x $4\frac{3}{4}$"h (14 cm x 12 cm)
With Blue, ch 12.
Work same as Front for 9 rows.
Finish off.

STITCH GUIDE

LONG DOUBLE CROCHET
(abbreviated LDC)
YO, working **around** previous two rows, insert hook in sc two rows **below** next ch-1, YO and pull up a loop even with last st made, (YO and draw through 2 loops on hook) twice ***(Fig. A)***.

Fig. A

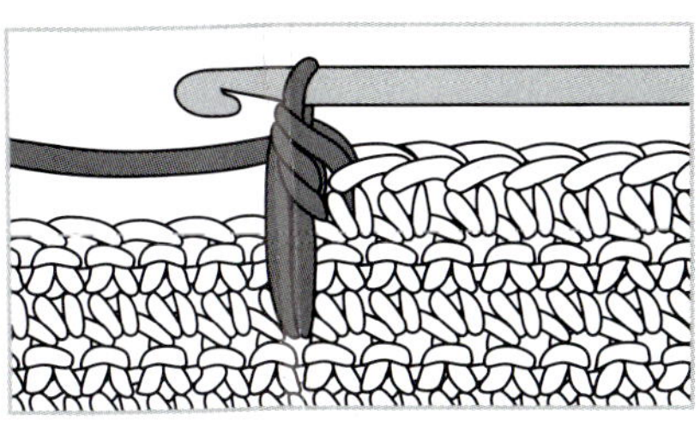

FRONT

With Blue, ch 28.

Row 1: Sc in second ch from hook and in each ch across changing to Brown in last sc made ***(Fig. 3, page 22)***: 27 sc.

Do **not** cut yarn; carry unused yarn **loosely** along side.

Row 2 (Right side)**:** Ch 3 **(counts as first dc, now and throughout)**, turn; dc in next 2 sc, ★ ch 1, skip next sc, dc in next 3 sc; repeat from ★ across: 21 dc and 6 ch-1 sps.

Note: Loop a short piece of yarn around any stitch to mark Row 2 as **right** side.

Row 3: Ch 1, turn; sc in first 3 dc, ★ ch 1, skip next ch, sc in next 3 dc; repeat ★ across changing to Blue in last sc made.

Row 4: Ch 1, turn; sc in first 3 sc, (work LDC, sc in next 3 sc) across: 21 sc and 6 LDC.

Row 5: Ch 1, turn; sc in each st across changing to Brown in last sc made: 27 sc.

Row 6: Ch 3, turn; dc in next 2 sc, ★ ch 1, skip next sc, dc in next 3 sc; repeat from ★ across: 21 dc and 6 ch-1 sps.

Repeat Rows 3-6 for pattern until piece measures approximately $14\frac{3}{4}$" (37.5 cm) from beginning ch, ending by working Row 4; cut Brown.

Edging: Ch 1, do **not** turn; work 25 sc evenly spaced across end of rows; working in free loops of beginning ch ***(Fig. 2, page 22)***, 3 sc in ch at base of first sc, sc in next ch and in each ch across to last ch, 3 sc in last ch; work 25 sc evenly spaced across end of rows; 3 sc in first sc, sc in each st across to last sc, 3 sc in last sc; join with slip st to first sc, finish off leaving a long end for sewing: 112 sc.

BACK

Work same as Front.

With **wrong** sides of Front and Back together, and working through **both** loops of **both** pieces, and using Blue, whipstitch pieces together along 3 sides ***(Fig. 5, page 23)***; insert pillow form, then whipstitch remaining side.

Design by Melissa Leapman.

PEEK-A-BOO PILLOW

An easy double crochet pattern in chunky yarn is the basis for this pillow. It's the multi-hued lining fabric peeking through the lacy look of the super-fast design that adds the visual interest needed to achieve home décor nirvana.

EASY

Finished Size: 14" (35.5 cm) square

MATERIALS

SUPER BULKY 6

- Super Bulky Weight Yarn [6 ounces, 106 yards (170 grams, 97 meters) per skein]: 2 skeins
- Crochet hook, size N (9 mm) **or** size needed for gauge
- 14" (35.5 cm) Pillow form
- Yarn needle

GAUGE: In pattern, 15 sts = 7" (17.75 cm);
4 rows = 4" (10 cm)

Gauge Swatch: 7"w x 3"h (17.75 cm x 7.5 cm)
Ch 17.
Work same as Front for 3 rows.
Finish off.

FRONT

Ch 29.

Row 1 (Right side)**:** Dc in fourth ch from hook and in next ch **(3 skipped chs count as first dc)**, ★ ch 1, skip next ch, dc in next 3 chs; repeat from ★ across: 21 dc and 6 ch-1 sps.

Note: Loop a short piece of yarn around any stitch to mark Row 1 as **right** side.

Row 2: Ch 4 **(counts as first dc plus ch 1)**, turn; skip next dc, dc in next dc, ★ dc in next ch-1 sp and in next dc, ch 1, skip next dc, dc in next dc; repeat from ★ across: 20 dc and 7 ch-1 sps.

Row 3: Ch 3 **(counts as first dc)**, turn; dc in next ch-1 sp and in next dc, ★ ch 1, skip next dc, dc in next dc, dc in next ch-1 sp and in next dc; repeat from ★ across: 21 dc and 6 ch-1 sps.

Repeat Rows 2 and 3 for pattern until Front measures approximately 13½" (34.5 cm) from beginning ch, ending by working Row 2; do **not** finish off.

Edging: Ch 1, turn; 3 sc in first dc, sc in each dc and in each ch-1 sp across to last dc, 3 sc in last dc; work 25 sc evenly spaced across end of rows; working in free loops of beginning ch ***(Fig. 2, page 22)***, 3 sc in first ch, sc in next 25 chs, 3 sc in next ch; work 25 sc evenly spaced across end of rows; join with slip st to first sc, finish off leaving a long end for sewing: 112 sc.

BACK

Work same as Front.

With **wrong** sides of Front and Back together and working through **both** loops of **both** pieces, whipstitch pieces together along 3 sides ***(Fig. 5, page 23)***; insert pillow form, then whipstitch remaining side.

Design by Lois J. Long.

DRAMATIC DIAMONDS PILLOW

Add texture and visual interest to any room with a little help from this Dramatic Diamonds Pillow. Front post treble stitches and front post treble cluster stitches in super-bulky weight yarn work up fast to create this dynamic design.

EASY +

Finished Size: 18" (45.5 cm) square

MATERIALS

Super Bulky Weight Yarn (SUPER BULKY 6)
[6 ounces, 106 yards (170 grams, 97 meters) per skein]:
4 skeins

Crochet hook, size N (9 mm) **or** size needed for gauge

18" (45.5 cm) Pillow form

Yarn needle

GAUGE: In pattern, 11 sts = 5½" (14 cm);
5 rows = 4¼" (10.75 cm)

Gauge Swatch: 5½"w x 4¼ "h
(14 cm x 10.75 cm)

Ch 12.

Work same as Front for 5 rows.

Finish off.

STITCH GUIDE

FRONT POST TREBLE CROCHET ***(abbreviated FPtr)***
YO twice, insert hook from **front** to **back** around post of st indicated ***(Fig. 1, page 22)***, YO and pull up a loop, (YO and draw through 2 loops on hook) 3 times.

FRONT POST TREBLE CROCHET CLUSTER ***(abbreviated FPtr Cluster)*** (uses 2 FPtr)
★ YO twice, insert hook from **front** to **back** around post of **next** FPtr one row **below** ***(Fig. 1, page 22)***, YO and pull up a loop, (YO and draw through 2 loops on hook) twice; repeat from ★ once **more**, YO and draw through all 3 loops on hook. Skip sc behind FPtr Cluster.

FRONT

Ch 36.

Row 1 (Right side)**:** Sc in second ch from hook and in each ch across: 35 sc.

Note: Loop a short piece of yarn around any stitch to mark Row 1 as **right** side.

Row 2: Ch 3 **(counts as first dc, now and throughout)**, turn; dc in next sc and in each sc across.

Row 3: Ch 3, turn; dc in next dc, skip next dc, work (FPtr, ch 1, FPtr) around next dc, ★ skip next dc, dc in next dc, skip next dc, work (FPtr, ch 1, FPtr) around next dc; repeat from ★ across to last 3 dc, skip next dc, dc in last 2 dc: 16 FPtr, 11 dc and 8 ch-1 sps.

Row 4: Ch 1, turn; sc in each st and in each ch-1 sp across: 35 sc.

Row 5: Ch 3, turn; dc in next 2 sc, (work FPtr Cluster, dc in next 3 sc) across.

Row 6: Ch 3, turn; dc in next dc and in each st across.

Row 7: Ch 3, turn; dc in next 3 dc, skip next dc, work (FPtr, ch 1, FPtr) around next dc, ★ skip next dc, dc in next dc, skip next dc, work (FPtr, ch 1, FPtr) around next dc; repeat from ★ across to last 5 dc, skip next dc, dc in last 4 dc: 14 FPtr, 14 dc and 7 ch-1 sps.

Row 8: Ch 1, turn; sc in each st and in each ch-1 sp across: 35 sc.

Row 9: Ch 3, turn; dc in next 4 sc, work FPtr Cluster, (dc in next 3 sc, work FPtr Cluster) across to last 5 sc, dc in last 5 sc.

Row 10: Ch 3, turn; dc in next dc and in each st across.

Rows 11-21: Repeat Rows 3-10 once, then repeat Rows 3-5 once **more**.

Row 22: Ch 1, turn; sc in each st across.

Edging: Ch 1, turn; 3 sc in first dc, sc in next dc and in each dc across to last dc, 3 sc in last dc; work 33 sc evenly spaced across end of rows; working in free loops of beginning ch ***(Fig. 2, page 22)***, 3 sc in first ch, sc in next 33 chs, 3 sc in next ch; work 33 sc evenly spaced across end of rows; join with slip st to first sc, finish off leaving a long end for sewing: 144 sc.

BACK

Work same as Front.

With **wrong** sides of Front and Back together and working through **both** loops of **both** pieces, whipstitch pieces together along 3 sides ***(Fig. 5, page 23)***; insert pillow form, then whipstitch remaining side.

Design by Lois J. Long.

BRILLIANT BOLSTER PILLOW

This design combines vibrant color, texture, and cables to create a smart pillow that's sure to make a statement on your sofa. Embellished with front post double and treble crochet stitches, it's the ideal fast and fabulous element you need to spruce up any setting.

INTERMEDIATE

Finished Size: 16" long x 8" diameter
(40.5 cm x 20.5 cm)

MATERIALS

SUPER BULKY 6

Super Bulky Weight Yarn
[6 ounces, 106 yards
(170 grams, 97 meters) per skein]:
3 skeins
Crochet hook, size N (9 mm) **or**
size needed for gauge
Pillow form - 8" x 16"
(20.5 cm x 40.5 cm)
Yarn needle

GAUGE: Rnds 1 and 2 of End = 2"
(5 cm) diameter
In Body pattern,
11 sts = 5½" (14 cm);
5 rnds = 2¾" (7 cm)

Gauge Swatch: 2" (5 cm) diameter
Work same as End through Rnd 2.
Do **not** finish off.

STITCH GUIDE

FRONT POST DOUBLE CROCHET ***(abbreviated FPdc)***
YO, insert hook from **front** to **back** around post of st indicated ***(Fig. 1, page 22)***, YO and pull up a loop (3 loops on hook), (YO and draw through 2 loops on hook) twice. Skip sc behind FPdc.

FRONT POST TREBLE CROCHET ***(abbreviated FPtr)***
YO twice, insert hook from **front** to **back** around post of st indicated ***(Fig. 1, page 22)***, YO and pull up a loop (4 loops on hook), (YO and draw through 2 loops on hook) 3 times.

CABLE (uses next 4 sts)
Skip next 2 sc, work FPtr around sts one rnd **below** next 2 sc, working in **front** of 2 FPtr just made, work FPtr around each st one rnd **below** 2 skipped sc. Skip 4 sc behind Cable.

END (Make 2)

Rnd 1 (Right side)**:** Ch 2, 6 sc in second ch from hook; do **not** join, place marker to mark beginning of rnd ***(see Markers, page 22)***.

Note: Loop a short piece of yarn around any stitch to mark Rnd 1 as **right** side.

Rnd 2: 2 Sc in each sc around: 12 sc.

Rnd 3: (Sc in next sc, 2 sc in next sc) around: 18 sc.

Rnd 4: (Sc in next 2 sc, 2 sc in next sc) around: 24 sc.

Rnd 5: (Sc in next 3 sc, 2 sc in next sc) around: 30 sc.

Rnd 6: (Sc in next 4 sc, 2 sc in next sc) around: 36 sc.

Rnd 7: (Sc in next 5 sc, 2 sc in next sc) around: 42 sc.

Rnd 8: (Sc in next 6 sc, 2 sc in next sc) around: 48 sc.

Rnd 9: (Sc in next 23 sc, 2 sc in next sc) twice: 50 sc.

Rnd 10: Sc in each sc around; slip st in next sc, finish off leaving a long end for sewing.

BODY

Ch 50; being careful **not** to twist ch, join with slip st to form a ring.

Rnd 1 (Right side)**:** Ch 3 **(counts as first dc)**, dc in next ch and in each ch around; join with slip st to first dc: 50 dc.

Note: Mark Rnd 1 as **right** side.

Rnd 2: Ch 1, turn; sc in same st and in each dc around; join with slip st to first sc.

Rnd 3: Ch 1, turn; sc in same st and in next sc, work FPdc around dc one rnd **below** next sc, sc in next 2 sc, ★ work Cable, sc in next 2 sc, work FPdc around dc one rnd **below** next sc, sc in next 2 sc; repeat from ★ around; join with slip st to first sc.

Rnd 4: Ch 1, turn; sc in same st and in each st around; join with slip st to first sc.

Rnd 5: Ch 1, turn; sc in same st and next sc, work FPdc around next FPdc one rnd **below**, sc in next 2 sc, ★ work FPdc around each of next 4 FPtr one rnd **below**, sc in next 2 sc, work FPdc around next FPdc one rnd **below**, sc in next 2 sc; repeat from ★ around; join with slip st to first sc.

Rnd 6: Ch 1, turn; sc in same st and in each st around; join with slip st to first sc.

Rnd 7: Ch 1, turn; sc in same st and in next sc, work FPdc around next FPdc one rnd **below**, sc in next 2 sc, ★ work Cable, sc in next 2 sc, work FPdc around next FPdc one rnd **below**, sc in next 2 sc; repeat from ★ around; join with slip st to first sc.

Repeat Rnds 4-7 for pattern until Body measures approximately 16" (40.5 cm) from beginning ch, ending by working Rnd 5.

Finish off.

ASSEMBLY

With **wrong** sides of one End and Body together and working through **both** loops of **both** pieces, whipstitch pieces together ***(Fig. 5, page 23)***. Insert pillow form, then whipstitch second End to Body in same manner.

Design by Lois J. Long.

FAB FLOWERS AFGHAN

The perfect portable project, you can work on the fun floral granny squares for this warm and cozy afghan just about anywhere. Plus, the quick and easy pattern is adjustable! Try transforming the large afghan design into a smaller throw or even a rug simply by subtracting squares.

EASY

Finished Size: 48" x 64" (122 cm x 162.5 cm)

MATERIALS

Super Bulky Weight Yarn SUPER BULKY 6
[6 ounces, 106 yards
(170 grams, 97 meters) per skein]:
- Dk Green - 11 skeins
- Ecru - 3 skeins
- Red, Orange, Lt Orange, Rust, **and** Yellow - 1 skein **each**

Crochet hook, size N (9 mm) **or** size needed for gauge
Yarn needle

GAUGE: Each Square = 8" (20.25 cm)

Gauge Swatch: 4" (10 cm)
Work same as Square through Rnd 2.

STITCH GUIDE

BEGINNING CLUSTER (uses one st)
Ch 2, ★ YO, insert hook in **same** st, YO and pull up a loop, YO and draw through 2 loops on hook; repeat from ★ once **more**, YO and draw through all 3 loops on hook.

CLUSTER (uses one sc)
YO, insert hook in next sc, YO and pull up a loop, YO and draw through 2 loops on hook, ★ YO, insert hook in **same** st, YO and pull up a loop, YO and draw through 2 loops on hook; repeat from ★ once **more**, YO and draw through all 4 loops on hook.

SQUARE (Make 48)

Make 12 **each**, working Rnd 2 in the following colors: Red, Orange, Lt Orange, **and** Rust.

With Yellow, ch 3; join with slip st to form a ring.

Rnd 1 (Right side)**:** Ch 1, 8 sc in ring; join with slip st to first sc, finish off.

Note: Loop a short piece of yarn around any stitch to mark Rnd 1 as **right** side.

Rnd 2: With **right** side facing, join next color with slip st in any sc; work beginning Cluster, ch 3, (work Cluster, ch 3) around; join with slip st to top of beginning Cluster, finish off: 8 ch-3 sps.

Rnd 3: With **right** side facing, join Dk Green with dc in any ch-3 sp ***(see Joining With Dc, page 22)***; (2 dc, ch 2, 3 dc) in same sp, 3 dc in next ch-3 sp, ★ (3 dc, ch 2, 3 dc) in next ch-3 sp, 3 dc in next ch-3 sp; repeat from ★ 2 times **more**; join with slip st to first dc, finish off: 36 dc and 4 ch-2 sps.

Rnd 4: With **right** side facing, join Ecru with sc in any ch-2 sp ***(see Joining With Sc, page 22)***; ch 2, sc in same sp, ch 1, skip next dc, (sc in next dc, ch 1, skip next dc) 4 times, ★ (sc, ch 2, sc) in next corner ch-2 sp, ch 1, skip next dc, (sc in next dc, ch 1, skip next dc) 4 times; repeat from ★ 2 times **more**; join with slip st to first sc, finish off: 24 sc and 24 sps.

Rnd 5: With **right** side facing, join Dk Green with dc in any corner ch-2 sp; (dc, ch 2, 2 dc) in same sp, 2 dc in each of next 5 ch-1 sps, ★ (2 dc, ch 2, 2 dc) in next corner ch-2 sp, 2 dc in each of next 5 ch-1 sps; repeat from ★ 2 times **more**; join with slip st to first dc, finish off: 56 dc and 4 ch-2 sps.

ASSEMBLY

With **wrong** sides together, working through **both** loops on **both** pieces, and using Dk Green, whipstitch Squares together ***(Fig. 5, page 23)***, forming 6 vertical strips of 8 Squares each, beginning in second ch of first corner ch-2 and ending in first ch of next corner ch-2; then whipstitch strips together in same manner.

TRIM

With **right** side facing, join Dk Green with sc in any corner ch-2 sp; sc evenly around entire afghan working 3 sc in each corner ch-2 sp; join with slip st to first sc, finish off.

Design by Maggie Weldon.

FLOWER GARDEN AFGHAN

Worked in strips made from an easy double crochet and chain combo, this lovely indoor flower garden is sure to warm up your environment while you dream of planting the real thing in the spring. Plus, finishing this afghan will feel like painting with yarn as you slip stitch the freehand stems and sew on the blossoms and leaves to your work of art.

EASY

Finished Size: 48" x 60" (122 cm x 152.5 cm)

MATERIALS

Super Bulky Weight Yarn [6 ounces, 106 yards (170 grams, 97 meters) per skein]:
- Ecru - 11 skeins
- Green - 7 skeins
- Red - 2 skeins
- Rose - 1 skein

Crochet hook, size N (9 mm) **or** size needed for gauge

Yarn needle

GAUGE: 9 dc = 4³/₄" (12 cm);
6 rows = 5¹/₂" (14 cm)
Each Panel = 6" wide (15.25 cm)

Gauge Swatch: 4³/₄"w x 5¹/₂"h (12 cm x 14 cm)
Work same as Panel Center for 6 rows.
Do **not** finish off.

PANEL (Make 8)

CENTER

With Ecru, ch 11.

Row 1 (Right side)**:** Dc in fourth ch from hook and in each ch across **(3 skipped chs count as first dc)**: 9 dc.

Note: Loop a short piece of yarn around any stitch to mark Row 1 as **right** side.

Rows 2-63: Ch 3, turn; dc in next dc and in each dc across.

Finish off.

Edging: With **right** side facing, join Green with dc in first dc on Row 63 ***(see Joining With Dc, page 22)***, (dc, ch 1, 2 dc) in same st, dc in next 7 dc, (2 dc, ch 1, 2 dc) in last dc; 2 dc in end of each row across; working in free loops of beginning ch ***(Fig. 2, page 22)***, (2 dc, ch 1, 2 dc) in first ch, dc in next 7 chs, (2 dc, ch 1, 2 dc) in next ch; 2 dc in end of each row across; join with slip st to first dc, finish off: 282 dc and 4 ch-1 sps.

Stem: With Green, make a slip knot, holding yarn to **wrong** side of Panel, working from bottom to top, insert hook in base of fourth dc on Row 1, hook loop and pull though st, using the diagram below as a guide, slip st evenly to top to form Stem; finish off.

FLOWER (Make 32)

With Red, ch 4; join with slip st to form a ring.

Rnd 1 (Right side)**:** (Ch 2, dc in ring, ch 2, slip st in ring) 5 times; finish off leaving a long end for sewing.

Note: Mark Rnd 1 as **right** side.

With Rose, add 3 French knots to center of Flower ***(Fig. 4, page 23)***.

LEAF (Make 32)

With Green, ch 5.

Row 1 (Right side)**:** Slip st in second ch from hook, sc in next 2 chs, (slip st, ch 1, slip st) in last ch; working in free loops of beginning ch, sc in next 2 chs, slip st in next ch; finish off leaving a long end for sewing.

Note: Mark Row 1 as **right** side.

Using diagram as a guide, sew 4 Flowers and 4 Leaves to each Panel.

With **wrong** sides together, working through **both** loops on **both** pieces, and using Green, whipstitch Panels together ***(Fig. 5, page 23)***.

Design by Maggie Weldon.

REALLY RIPPLES LAP-GHAN

Flowing lines, great texture, and endless color options can quickly be yours with this simply stylish lap afghan. Quick to complete using chunky yarn and a combination of easy double crochet stitches in a repeating pattern, it's surely destined to be the just-right accessory for your refuge.

EASY

Finished Size: 30" x 42" (76 cm x 106.5 cm)

MATERIALS

Super Bulky Weight Yarn [6 ounces, 106 yards (170 grams, 97 meters) per skein]: 7 skeins

Crochet hook, size N (9 mm) **or** size needed for gauge

GAUGE: In pattern, one repeat (from point to point) = 7 1/2" (19 cm); 3 rows = 3 1/2" (9 cm)

Gauge swatch: 15"w x 3 1/2"h (38 cm x 9 cm)
Ch 41.
Work same as Lap Afghan for 3 rows.
Finish off.

STITCH GUIDE

BEGINNING DECREASE (uses next 2 dc)
★ YO, insert hook in **next** dc, YO and pull up a loop, YO and draw through 2 loops on hook; repeat from ★ once **more**, YO and draw through all 3 loops on hook **(counts as one dc)**.

DECREASE (uses next 3 sts)
★ YO, insert hook in **next** st, YO and pull up a loop, YO and draw through 2 loops on hook; repeat from ★ 2 times **more**, YO and draw through all 4 loops on hook **(counts as one dc)**.

ENDING DECREASE (uses last 3 dc)
★ YO, insert hook in **next** dc, YO and pull up a loop, YO and draw through 2 loops on hook; repeat from ★ once **more**, YO, insert hook in last dc, YO and pull up a loop, YO and draw 2 loops on hook, YO and draw through all 4 loops on hook **(counts as one dc)**.

LAP-GHAN

Ch 85.

Row 1 (Right side)**:** Dc in fourth ch from hook and in next 6 chs **(3 skipped chs count as first dc)**, dc in next ch, (ch 1, dc in same st) twice, ★ dc in next 8 chs, skip next ch, decrease, skip next ch, dc in next 8 chs, dc in next ch, (ch 1, dc in same st) twice; repeat from ★ 2 times **more**, dc in next 8 chs: 79 dc and 8 ch-1 sps.

Note: Loop a short piece of yarn around any stitch to mark Row 1 as **right** side.

Row 2: Ch 2, turn; work beginning decrease, dc in next 6 dc and in next ch-1 sp, dc in next dc, (ch 1, dc in same st) twice, ★ dc in next ch-1 sp and in next 7 dc, skip next dc, decrease, skip next dc, dc in next 7 dc and in next ch-1 sp, dc in next dc, (ch 1, dc in same st) twice; repeat from ★ across to last ch-1 sp, dc in last ch-1 sp and in next 6 dc, work ending decrease.

Repeat Row 2 for pattern until Lap-ghan measures approximately 42" (106.5 cm) from beginning ch, ending by working a **right** side row; finish off.

Design by Renee D. Chapman.

WINDOWPANE AFGHAN

Paired with its matching pillow, this long double crochet-accented lap afghan is a fast-to-finish must-have. Drape it over your sofa for a stylish addition to your haven that also doubles as a cozy cover-up for lounging around.

EASY +

Finished Size: 33" x 43½" (84 cm x 110.5 cm)

MATERIALS

SUPER BULKY 6

Super Bulky Weight Yarn
[6 ounces, 106 yards
(170 grams, 97 meters) per skein]:
- Brown - 5 skeins
- Blue - 4 skeins

Crochet hook, size N (9 mm) **or** size needed for gauge

GAUGE: In pattern, 11 sts = 5½" (14 cm);
9 rows = 4¾" (12 cm)

Gauge swatch: 5½"w x 4¾" h (14 cm x 12 cm)
With Brown, ch 12.
Work same as Body for 9 rows.
Finish off.

STITCH GUIDE

LONG DOUBLE CROCHET ***(abbreviated LDC)***

YO, working **around** previous two rows, insert hook in sc two rows **below** next ch-1, YO and pull up a loop even with last st made, (YO and draw through 2 loops on hook) twice ***(Fig. A, page 3)***.

BODY

With Brown, ch 64.

Row 1: Sc in second ch from hook and in each ch across changing to Blue in last sc made ***(Fig. 3, page 22)***: 63 sc.

Do **not** cut yarn, carry unused yarn **loosely** along edge.

Row 2 (Right side)**:** Ch 3 **(counts as first dc, now and throughout)**, turn; dc in next 2 sc, ★ ch 1, skip next sc, dc in next 3 sc; repeat from ★ across: 48 dc and 15 ch-1 sps.

Note: Loop a short piece of yarn around any stitch to mark Row 2 as **right** side.

Row 3: Ch 1, turn; sc in first 3 dc, ★ ch 1, skip next ch, sc in next 3 dc; repeat ★ across changing to Brown in last sc made.

Row 4: Ch 1, turn; sc in first 3 sc, (work LDC, sc in next 3 sc) across: 48 sc and 15 LDC.

Row 5: Ch 1, turn; sc in each st across changing to Blue in last sc made: 63 sc.

Row 6: Ch 3, turn; dc in next 2 sc, ★ ch 1, skip next sc, dc in next 3 sc; repeat from ★ across: 48 dc and 15 ch-1 sps.

Repeat Rows 3-6 for pattern until Body measures approximately 42" (105.5 cm) from beginning ch, ending by working Row 4; cut Blue.

EDGING

Rnd 1: Ch 1, do **not** turn; sc evenly around entire Body working 3 sc in each corner; join with slip st to first sc.

Rnd 2: Ch 1, working from **left** to **right**, work reverse sc in same st and in each sc around ***(Figs. 6a-d, page 23)***; join with slip st to first st, finish off.

Design by Melissa Leapman.

OCTAGON AFGHAN

Geometric flair combined with a splash of vibrant color makes this afghan a striking addition to any décor. A great take-along project, the quick-to-complete design is worked in motifs, squares, and triangles that are whipstitched together and edged with a simple border.

EASY

Finished Size: 49½" x 69" (125.5 cm x 175.5 cm)

MATERIALS

SUPER BULKY 6

Super Bulky Weight Yarn
[6 ounces, 106 yards
(170 grams, 97 meters) per skein]:
- Brown - 14 skeins
- Green - 6 skeins

Crochet hook, size N (9 mm) **or** size needed for gauge
Yarn needle

GAUGE: Each Motif = 6½" (16.5 cm) across

Gauge Swatch: 3" (7.5 cm)
Work same as Square.

STITCH GUIDE

TREBLE CROCHET *(abbreviated tr)*
YO twice, insert hook in st indicated, YO and pull up a loop (4 loops on hook), (YO and draw through 2 loops on hook) 3 times.

MOTIF (Make 70)

With Brown, ch 6; join with slip st to form a ring.

Rnd 1 (Right side)**:** Ch 3 **(counts as first dc, now and throughout)**, 15 dc in ring; join with slip st to first dc, finish off: 16 dc.

Note: Loop a short piece of yarn around any stitch to mark Rnd 1 as **right** side.

Rnd 2: With **right** side facing, join Green with dc in any dc **before** joining ***(see Joining With Dc, page 22)***; skip next dc, tr in next dc, working **behind** tr just made, dc in skipped dc, place marker in dc just worked into, ★ tr in next dc, working **behind** tr just made and to right of previous tr, dc in same st as previous tr; repeat from ★ 12 times **more**, tr in same st as first tr to left of dc, working **behind** tr just made and to right of previous tr, dc in same st as previous tr, tr in marked st to left of dc; remove marker; join with slip st to first dc, finish off: 32 sts.

Rnd 3: With **right** side facing, join Brown with dc in same st as joining; dc in next tr, (dc, ch 1, dc) in next dc, ★ dc in next 3 sts, (dc, ch 1, dc) in next dc; repeat from ★ around to last tr, dc in last tr; join with slip st to first dc, finish off: 40 dc and 8 ch-1 sps.

SQUARE (Make 54)

With Brown, ch 3; join with slip st to form a ring.

Rnd 1 (Right side)**:** Ch 3, 2 dc in ring, ch 3, (3 dc in ring, ch 3) 3 times; join with slip st to first dc, finish off: 12 dc and 4 ch-3 sps.

Note: Mark Rnd 1 as **right** side.

TRIANGLE (Make 30)

With Brown, ch 5; join with slip st to form a ring.

Row 1 (Right side)**:** Ch 5 **(counts as first tr plus ch 1)**, (3 dc, ch 3, 3 dc) in ring, ch 1, tr in ch **before** joining; finish off: 8 sts and 3 sps.

Note: Mark Rnd 1 as **right** side.

Instructions continued on page 20.

ASSEMBLY

With Brown, using Placement Diagram as a guide, and working in **both** loops on both pieces, whipstitch Motifs together ***(Fig. 5, page 23)***, forming 7 vertical strips of 10 Motifs each, beginning in first corner ch-1 and ending in next corner ch-1.

Whipstitch 9 Squares to first strip matching corner ch-1 to center ch of corner ch-3 of Square; then whipstitch second strip to first strip. Continue joining Squares and strips in same manner.

Whipstitch Triangles to outer edges, beginning in first tr on Triangle **and** in corner ch-1 on Motif and ending in last tr on Triangle **and** corresponding center ch on next Motif.

PLACEMENT DIAGRAM

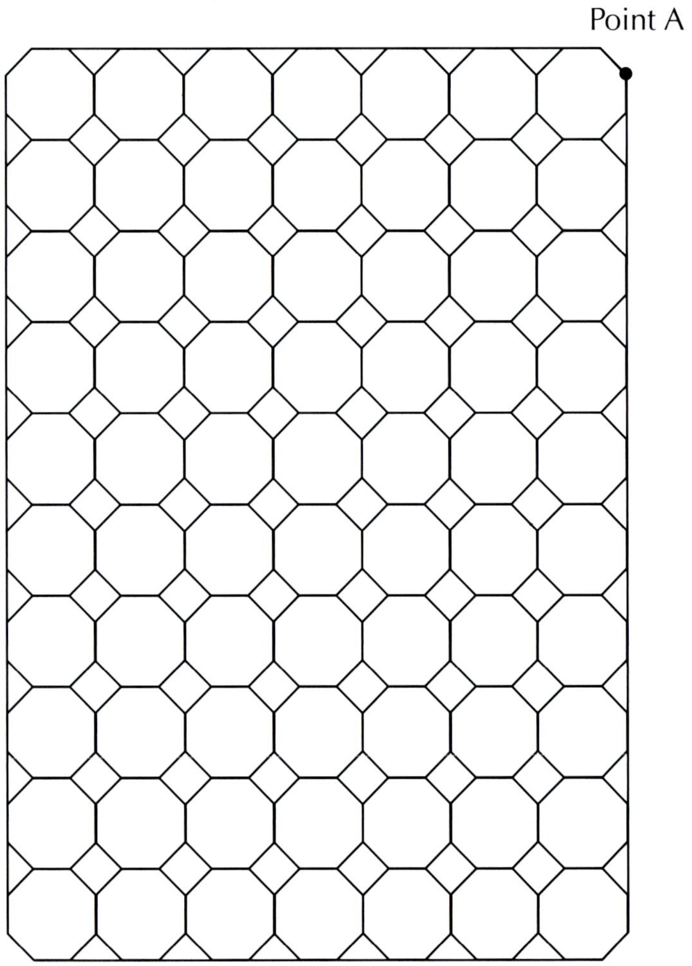

EDGING

Rnd 1: With **right** side facing, join Brown with slip st in ch-1 sp at Point A on Placement Diagram; ch 4 **(counts as first dc plus ch 1)**, place marker around dc just made for st placement, ★ † dc in next dc, ch 1, (skip next dc, dc in next dc, ch 1) twice, dc in next ch-1 sp, ch 1, dc in next dc, ch 1, (skip next dc, dc in next dc, ch 1) twice, ♥ working in end of rows on next Triangle, sc in top of next tr, ch 1, sc in base of same tr, ch 1, sc in base of next tr, ch 1, sc in top of same tr, ch 1, skip next joining; working across next motif, dc in next dc, ch 1, (skip next dc, dc in next dc, ch 1) twice ♥, repeat from ♥ to ♥ across to next corner ch-1 sp †, dc in next ch-1 sp, place marker around dc just made for st placement, ch 1; repeat from ★ 2 times **more**, then repeat from † to † once; join with slip st to first dc.

Rnd 2: (Ch 1, sc in next ch-1 sp) 4 times, ★ † ch 2, sc in next ch-1 sp, (ch 1, sc in next ch-1 sp) across to next marked st, ch 2 †, sc in next ch-1 sp, (ch 1, sc in next ch-1 sp) 3 times; repeat from ★ 2 times **more**, then repeat from † to † once; join with slip st to first sc.

Rnd 3: Ch 1, ★ (sc in next ch-1 sp, ch 1) across to next ch-2 sp, (sc, ch 1) twice in ch-2 sp; repeat from ★ around; join with slip st to first sc.

Rnd 4: (Slip in next ch-1 sp, ch 1) around; join with slip st to first slip st, finish off.

Design by Anne Halliday.

GENERAL INSTRUCTIONS

ABBREVIATIONS

ch(s) chain
cm centimeters
dc double crochet
FPdc Front Post double crochet(s)
FPtr Front Post treble crochet(s)
LDC Long Double Crochet(s)
mm millimeters
Rnd(s) round(s)
sc single crochet
sp(s) space(s)
st(s) stitch(es)
tr treble crochet(s)
YO yarn over

★ — work instructions following ★ as many **more** times as indicated in addition to the first time.

† to † or ♥ to ♥ — work all instructions from first † to second † or first ♥ to second ♥ **as many** times as specified.

( ) or [ ] — work enclosed instructions **as many** times as specified by the number immediately following **or** work all enclosed instructions in the stitch or space indicated **or** contains explanatory remarks.

colon (:) — the number(s) given after a colon at the end of a row or round denote(s) the number of stitches or spaces you should have on that row or round.

CROCHET TERMINOLOGY		
UNITED STATES		INTERNATIONAL
slip stitch (slip st)	=	single crochet (sc)
single crochet (sc)	=	double crochet (dc)
half double crochet (hdc)	=	half treble crochet (htr)
double crochet (dc)	=	treble crochet(tr)
treble crochet (tr)	=	double treble crochet (dtr)
double treble crochet (dtr)	=	triple treble crochet (ttr)
triple treble crochet (tr tr)	=	quadruple treble crochet (qtr)
skip	=	miss

Yarn Weight Symbol & Names	LACE 0	SUPER FINE 1	FINE 2	LIGHT 3	MEDIUM 4	BULKY 5	SUPER BULKY 6
Type of Yarns in Category	Fingering, 10-count crochet thread	Sock, Fingering Baby	Sport, Baby	DK, Light Worsted	Worsted, Afghan, Aran	Chunky, Craft, Rug	Bulky, Roving
Crochet Gauge* Ranges in Single Crochet to 4" (10 cm)	32-42 double crochets**	21-32 sts	16-20 sts	12-17 sts	11-14 sts	8-11 sts	5-9 sts
Advised Hook Size Range	Steel*** 6,7,8 Regular hook B-1	B-1 to E-4	E-4 to 7	7 to I-9	I-9 to K-10.5	K-10.5 to M-13	M-13 and larger

*GUIDELINES ONLY: The chart above reflects the most commonly used gauges and hook sizes for specific yarn categories.

** Lace weight yarns are usually crocheted on larger-size hooks to create lacy openwork patterns. Accordingly, a gauge range is difficult to determine. Always follow the gauge stated in your pattern.

*** Steel crochet hooks are sized differently from regular hooks–the higher the number the smaller the hook, which is the reverse of regular hook sizing.

CROCHET HOOKS													
U.S.	B-1	C-2	D-3	E-4	F-5	G-6	H-8	I-9	J-10	K-10 $^1/_2$	N	P	Q
Metric - mm	2.25	2.75	3.25	3.5	3.75	4	5	5.5	6	6.5	9	10	15

BEGINNER	Projects for first-time crocheters using basic stitches. Minimal shaping.
EASY	Projects using yarn with basic stitches, repetitive stitch patterns, simple color changes, and simple shaping and finishing.
INTERMEDIATE	Projects using a variety of techniques, such as basic lace patterns or color patterns, mid-level shaping and finishing.
EXPERIENCED	Projects with intricate stitch patterns, techniques and dimension, such as non-repeating patterns, multi-color techniques, fine threads, small hooks, detailed shaping and refined finishing.

GAUGE

Exact gauge is **essential** for proper size. Before beginning your project, make the sample swatch given in the individual instructions in the yarn and hook specified. After completing the swatch, measure it, counting your stitches and rows or rounds carefully. If your swatch is larger or smaller than specified, **make another, changing hook size to get the correct gauge**. Keep trying until you find the size hook that will give you the specified gauge.

MARKERS

Markers are used to help distinguish the beginning of each round being worked. Place a 2" (5 cm) scrap piece of yarn before the first stitch of each round, moving marker after each round is complete.

JOINING WITH SC

When instructed to join with sc, begin with a slip knot on hook. Insert hook in stitch or space indicated, YO and pull up a loop, YO and draw through both loops on hook.

JOINING WITH DC

When instructed to join with dc, begin with a slip knot on hook. YO, holding loop on hook, insert hook in stitch or space indicated, YO and pull up a loop (3 loops on hook), (YO and draw through 2 loops on hook) twice.

POST STITCH

Work around post of stitch indicated, inserting hook in direction of arrow ***(Fig. 1)***.

Fig. 1

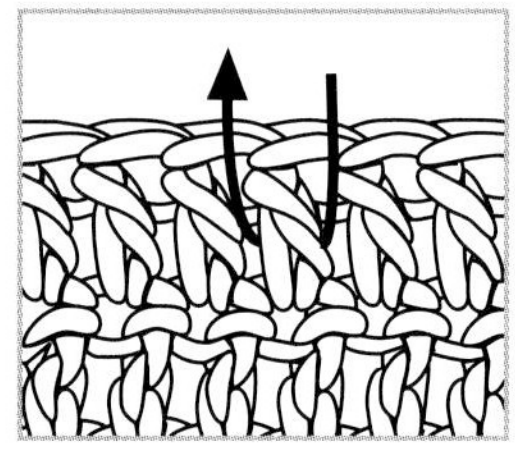

FREE LOOPS OF A CHAIN

When instructed to work in free loops of a chain, work in loop indicated by arrow ***(Fig. 2)***.

Fig. 2

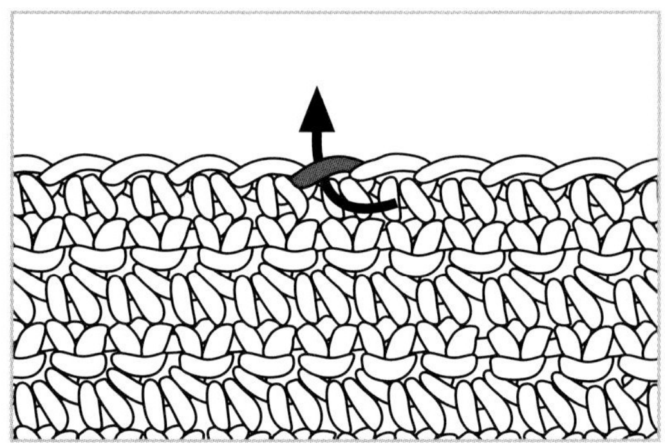

CHANGING COLORS

Work the last stitch to within one step of completion, hook new yarn ***(Fig. 3)*** and draw through all loops on hook. Do **not** cut yarn until instructed.

Fig. 3

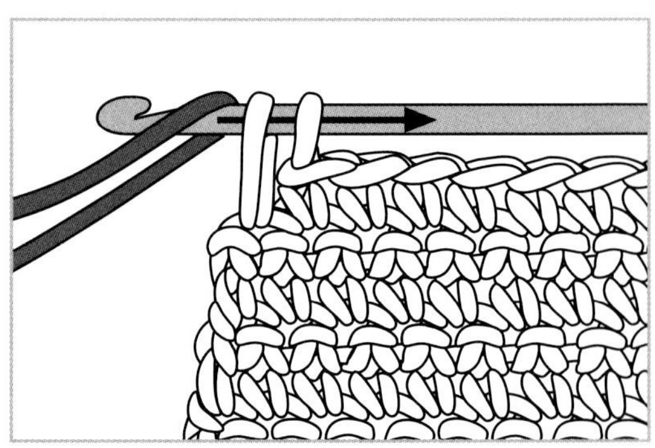

FRENCH KNOT

Bring needle up at 1. Wrap yarn around the needle the desired number of times and insert needle at 2, holding end of yarn with non-stitching fingers ***(Fig. 4)***. Tighten knot; then pull needle through, holding yarn until it must be released.

Fig. 4

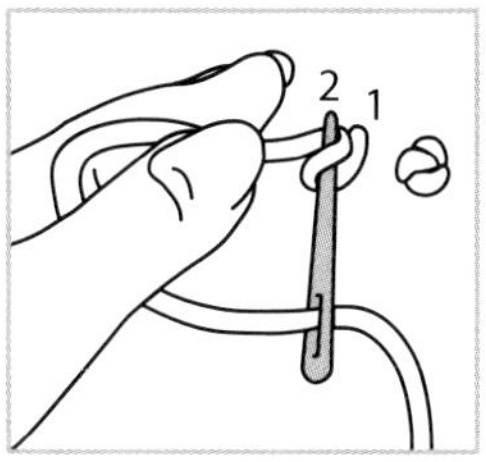

WHIPSTITCH

Place two Motifs, Squares or Panels with **wrong** sides together. Sew through both pieces once to secure the beginning of the seam, leaving an ample yarn end to weave in later. Insert the needle from **front** to **back** through **both** loops on **both** pieces ***(Fig. 5)***. Bring the needle around and insert it from **front** to **back** through next loops on both pieces. Continue in this manner across, keeping the sewing yarn fairly loose.

Fig. 5

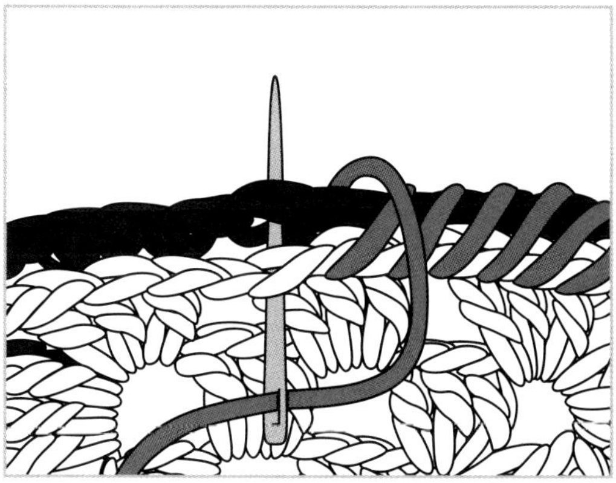

REVERSE SINGLE CROCHET

(abbreviated reverse sc)

Working from **left** to **right**, ★ insert hook in st to right of hook ***(Fig. 6a)***, YO and draw through, under and to left of loop on hook (2 loops on hook) ***(Fig. 6b)***, YO and draw through both loops on hook ***(Fig. 6c)*** **(reverse sc made, *Fig. 6d*)**; repeat from ★ around.

Fig. 6a

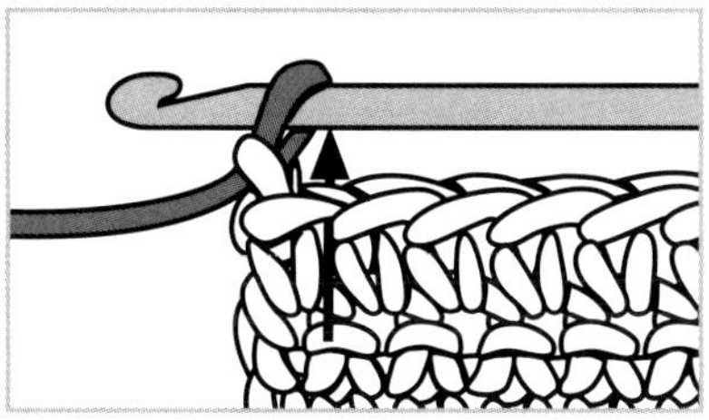

Fig. 6b

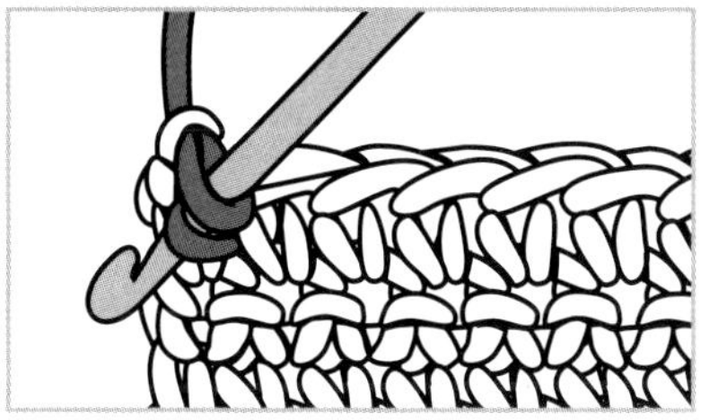

Fig. 6c

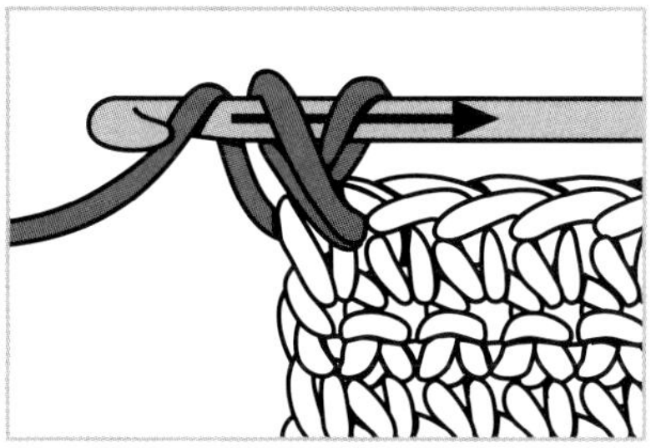

Fig. 6d

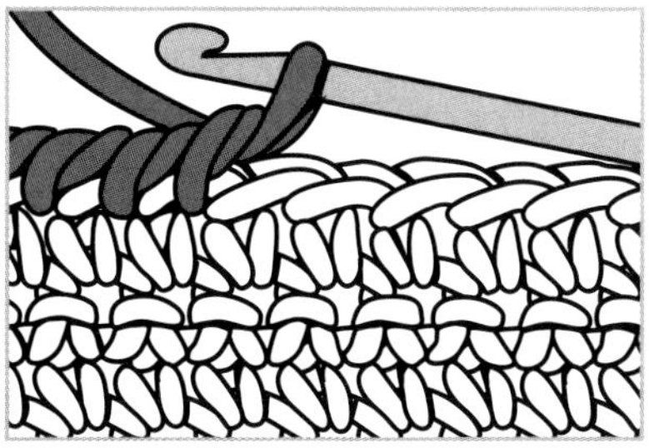

YARN INFORMATION

Each project in this leaflet was made using Lion Brand® Wool-Ease® Thick & Quick®. Any brand of Super Bulky Weight Yarn may be used. It is best to refer to the yardage/meters when determining how many balls or skeins to purchase. Remember, to arrive at the finished size, it is the GAUGE/TENSION that is important, not the brand of yarn.

For your convenience, listed below are the specific colors used to create our photography models.

WINDOWPANE PILLOW
Blue - #106 Sky Blue
Brown - #404 Wood

PEEK-A-BOO PILLOW
#404 Wood

DRAMATIC DIAMONDS PILLOW
#106 Sky Blue

BRILLIANT BOLSTER PILLOW
#132 Lemongrass

FAB FLOWERS AFGHAN
Dk Green - #131 Grass
Ecru - #099 Fisherman
Red - #138 Cranberry
Orange - #133 Pumpkin
Lt Orange - #189 Butterscotch
Rust - #135 Spice
Yellow - #134 Citron

FLOWER GARDEN AFGHAN
Ecru - #099 Fisherman
Green - #131 Grass
Red - #138 Cranberry
Rose - #112 Raspberry

REALLY RIPPLE LAP-GHAN
#099 Fisherman

WINDOWPANE AFGHAN
Brown - #404 Wood
Blue - #106 Sky Blue

OCTAGON AFGHAN
Brown - #404 Wood
Green - #132 Lemongrass

Production Team: Instructional Editor - Lois J. Long; Technical Editor - Sarah J. Green; Editorial Writer - Susan McManus Johnson; Senior Graphic Artist - Lora Puls; Graphic Artist - Dana Vaughn; Photo Stylist - Sondra Daniel; and Photographer - Ken West.